THE GEOGRAPHY DETECTIVE
INVESTIGATES
Mountains

Jen Green

WAYLAND

First published in 2007 by Wayland

Copyright © Wayland 2007

Editor: Hayley Fairhead
Designer: Simon Morse
Maps and artwork: Peter Bull
Cartoon artwork: Richard Hook

Wayland
338 Euston Road
London NW1 3BH

Wayland
Hachette Children's Books
Level 17/207 Kent Street
Sydney, NSW 2000

Green, Jen
    Mountains. - (The geography detective investigates)
    1. Mountains - Juvenile literature
    I. Title
    551.4'32

ISBN 978-0-7502-5048-1

Printed in China

Wayland is a division of Hachette Children's Books.

Picture acknowledgements: Tony West/Corbis: cover, Macduff Everton/Corbis: 1, David Paterson/Wild Country/Corbis; 4, Galen Rowell/Corbis: 5, Lester Lefkowitz/Corbis: 6, Macduff Everton/Corbis: 7t, Claes Axstal/Superbild/A1Pix: 7b, Frank Lukassech/zefa/Corbis: 8, Joseph Sohm/Corbis: 9, Nawang Sherpa/Bogati/Zuma/Corbis: 11, Craig Tuttle/Corbis: 13, Fritz Polking/Ecoscene: 14, Galen Rowell/Corbis: 15, Anders Ryman/Corbis: 16, Robert Holmes/Corbis; 17, Craig Aurness/Corbis: 18, Adam Woolfitt/Corbis: 19, Keren Su/Corbis: 20, Preston Schlebusch/Image bank/GettyImages: 21t, Richard List/Corbis: 21b, David Samuel Robbins/Corbis: 22, Ellen Schuster/Image bank/GettyImages: 23, Olivier Maire/epa/Corbis: 24, Steve Terrill/Corbis: 25, Joe Cornish/NTPL: 26, John C. Dornkamp/Alamy: 27, Tony West/Corbis: 28, Derek Middleton/FLPA/Corbis: 29.

Cover: a couple enjoy the mountain scenery in the Lake District, England.

Contents

Words that appear in **bold** can be
found in the glossary on page 30.

Answers to Sherlock Bones'
questions can be found on page 31.

What are mountains?

Mountains are steep-sided uplands rising more than 500 m above the surrounding **lowlands**. Lower areas of high ground are called hills. Most mountains are found in groups called **ranges**, and some form long chains running for hundreds of kilometres. Mountains are found on every continent, and even rise from the ocean bed.

Ben Nevis, Britain's highest peak, is 1,343 m tall.

Mountains are colder than low level ground because the air is thinner (less dense) the higher you go. The thin air can hold less of the sun's heat. In fact, the temperature drops 1°C for every 150 m you climb. The higher up you go, the colder the climate and the more unusual plants you find growing there. Certain animals are also suited to life in this cold environment.

FOCUS ON

Record-breaking mountains

The Himalayas in Asia are the world's highest mountains. Mount Everest is the tallest peak at 8,848 m high. The Andes, which runs for more than 7,000 km, is the longest mountain range in the world.

Urals

Alps

Rockies

Pyrenees

Appalachians

Atlas

Himalayas

Mid-Indian
Ridge

Andes

Mid-Atlantic
Ridge

The map shows some
of the world's highest
mountain ranges.

Fewer people live in mountains than in lowland areas.
However, mountain villages and towns have grown up in
areas sheltered from winds and colder temperatures.
Most mountain people traditionally lived by farming or
keeping animals. Mountains are also mined for useful
minerals, and in the last 50 years tourism has become
big business. Some of these activities have harmed
mountain environments, but now we are
learning to take better care of
mountains and their wildlife.

In the Alps, summer daytime
temperatures average 32°C in
valleys at 1,000 m. The highest
peaks are 4,800 m. What is the
average temperature at the top?

Mountains can be sacred places. Buddhists
make a pilgrimage to Mount Kailas in Tibet,
believed to be the home of the gods.

How do mountains form?

Just 50 years ago, no one knew much about the mighty forces that create mountains. Now we know that they are formed by the movements of huge sections of the Earth's surface, called **tectonic** plates, that make up Earth's outer **crust**. These giant rigid sections float on the red-hot, **molten** layer below the crust and slowly drift across Earth's surface, moving at 1-3 cm a year. As they drift, they slowly collide, pull apart, or scrape past one another.

There are three main types of mountains: **fold mountains**, volcanoes and **fault-block mountains**. All three are formed in different ways. Fold mountains form when tectonic plates crash together on land. The collision zone buckles upward to create a **range** of mountains. The Himalayas and Alps both formed in this way.

Where tectonic plates scrape past each other, the tremendous pressure causes the rocks to break. Deep cracks called **faults** are found near plate edges. In some areas a slab of rock between two faults is forced upward to form a fault-block mountain. The Vosges mountains in France and the Basin and Range mountains in the USA are fault-block mountains.

The Basin and Range mountains, USA, are fault-block mountains.

The Himalayas are fold mountains that began to form about 45 million years ago.

Volcanoes occur where red-hot rock from deep underground bursts through a weak point in the crust. The erupted rock, called **lava**, builds up and hardens to form a steep-sided mountain. Volcanoes also erupt on the ocean bed. Eventually the mountain of lava rises above the sea to form an island. The islands of Hawaii are a chain of volcanoes rising from the bed of the Pacific Ocean.

Can you explain why Mount Fuji is cone-shaped?

Mount Fuji, Japan's highest peak, is a volcano.

How are mountains shaped?

Mountains are worn down by natural forces such as wind, ice and water. Over millions of years, high craggy mountains are worn into smooth, rounded shapes. This process is called **erosion**.

Ice and water are the main forces at work shaping mountains. Water trickling into cracks in rocks freezes at night. The ice expands to split the rocks, which collect in heaps called **scree**. Streams rushing downhill carve steep, V-shaped **gullies** and **gorges**. They carry earth and rocks downstream.

Glaciers flowing downward carve deep, U-shaped valleys in high mountains. Where several glaciers flow side by side, they can carve pointed peaks or steep ridges. Ice lying in hollows gouge out small, round lakes called **corries**.

FOCUS ON

Reading maps

The rising shapes of mountains are shown on maps using marks called contour lines. These lines join places at the same height above sea level. The closer the contour lines, the steeper the mountain. Forests, cliffs, paths and villages are also marked on maps.

The steep-sided peak of the Matterhorn in the Alps was carved by glaciers flowing down on all sides.

How do you think Red Tarn below Helvellyn was formed?

DETECTIVE WORK

Imagine you are climbing Helvellyn from the village of Glenridding. There are several ways up. Study the map, choose a route and then describe the features you pass.

In Yosemite Park, USA, a glacier carved a deep, U-shaped valley. Smaller glaciers created 'hanging valleys' above the main valley. Waterfalls spill over the steep cliffs.

In the bottom left of this map you will see the top of Helvellyn, a mountain in the English Lake District. It has steep ridges around it.

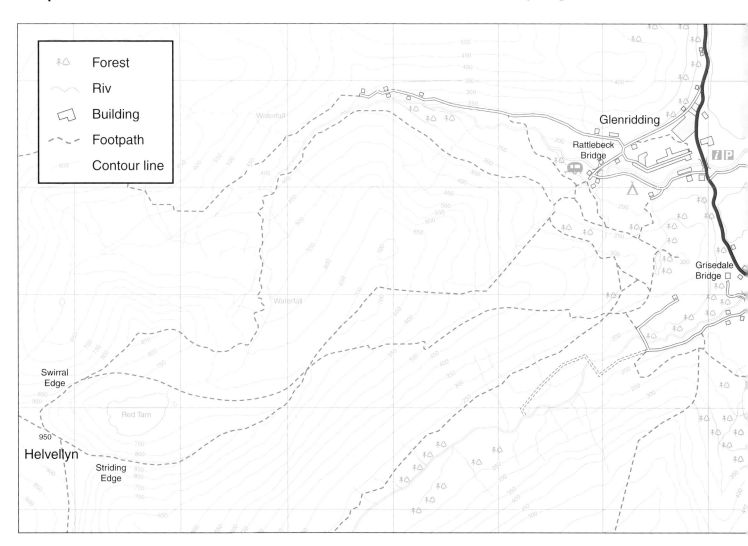

Legend:
- Forest
- Riv
- Building
- Footpath
- Contour line

Glenridding
Rattlebeck Bridge
Grisedale Bridge
Swirral Edge
Red Tarn
Helvellyn
Striding Edge
Waterfall

What is mountain weather like?

Mountain winters are long and icy. Snow blankets the ground and gathers in deep drifts. Summers are short because spring comes late, and autumn early. However, in hot countries the cool of the mountains can be welcome after the heat of the **lowlands**.

Rain falls on slopes facing wet ocean winds.

Prevailing wind

Rain shadow area

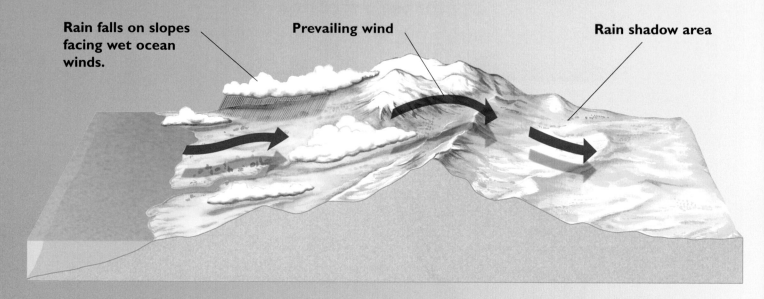

The diagram shows the rainfall pattern on a mountain. Slopes facing the wind are wettest, while the far side of the mountain, called the rain shadow area, is very dry.

Different parts of a mountain have different conditions. Sunny slopes are warmest, while snow lingers in shady areas. Slopes facing the wind are wettest. This is because warm, moist air rises from the ocean. As it meets the mountain, it cools, and the moisture **condenses** to form clouds that shed rain or snow.

Mountains are some of the windiest places on earth. Temperature differences at various heights get the air moving, creating strong winds. The wind quickly brings all kinds of weather: including sunshine, showers, mist, snow, hail and thunderstorms. It is often said that in the mountains, you can experience all four seasons in a single day!

FOCUS ON

Extreme conditions

On high mountain summits, the air is so thin that climbers use bottled oxygen. The region above 8,000 m is known as the 'death zone' because no one can survive there for long.

What clothing would you need on a hike in high mountains? Think about all the weather conditions you might meet.

These climbers are prepared for the extreme conditions found on high mountain peaks.

When you go on a mountain hike you need to prepare for all sorts of weather. You need to take a compass in case the mist comes down, a first-aid kit, spare food and plenty of water. It is always best to hike with a group of people and to let someone at the bottom of the mountain know where you are going.

What plants grow on mountains?

Plants have to adapt to grow in high mountain areas. The soil is thin and stony, and may be frozen for much of the year. Plants have to cope with strong winds and months of frost, ice and snow. Surprisingly, they may also have to survive very dry conditions, because ice and snow provide little moisture until they melt.

The increasing cold experienced as you go up the mountain creates a series of zones where different plants can grow. At the base of the mountain, the vegetation is similar to the **lowlands**. Broadleaved trees thrive in mild and tropical regions. Higher up, the only trees are conifers. Their narrow leaves hold moisture and remain on the tree all year. Higher still, no trees grow beyond a zone called the tree line. Above the tree line, grasses, flowering plants and mosses flourish in alpine **pastures** and meadows. Ground above the snow line is covered with ice and snow all year round, so there is little plant life there.

This diagram shows the vegetation zones found at different heights on a mountain.

Snow line

Alpine pasture

Tree line

Conifer belt

Broadleaved forest belt

DETECTIVE WORK

Hike to your nearest hill or mountain with a group of people. Take photos or make drawings of the plants you see. What special features do the plants have that make them suited to their mountain environment?

The growing season on mountains is short. As soon as the snow melts, plants flower and then quickly set seed before the chill of autumn returns. In winter, plants die back and survive as bulbs or **tubers** in the soil until spring comes.

You can see the mountain vegetation zones in this picture. In spring and summer, these meadows are carpeted with flowers.

FOCUS ON

Hardy alpines

Plants on high pastures are called alpines. Many have long roots to gather moisture. Some alpines grow in low clumps that provide shelter from icy winds. Beyond the snow line the only living things are splashes of lichen growing on rocks.

How do animals live on mountains?

Like plants, mountain animals have special features to help them cope with their harsh habitat. Some birds have extra feathers, while mammals from large yaks to marmots have thick fur to keep warm. Mammals such as Andean llamas have extra-large hearts and lungs to cope with the thin air. Sheep and goat-antelope called chamois have non-slip hooves that allow them to walk over bare rock.

Many mountain animals are fair-weather visitors. In spring, sheep and chamois move up to graze on the high **pastures**. In winter, they drop down to sheltered forests. Predators such as lynx, wolves and snow leopards move up and down the mountain after their prey.

Snow leopards are very rare animals. They prey on sheep and goats in the Himalayas.

A few animals remain high up all year round. In North America, rat-sized mammals called pikas store hay to provide food for winter. Marmots, dormice and snakes retire to their burrows and pass the winter months in the deep sleep of hibernation. In spring, they become active again.

The relationships between living things in a habitat are shown in diagrams called food chains. In the Himalayas, grass provides food for blue sheep. Sheep may be killed and eaten by a snow leopard. When animals die, their bodies are broken down by scavengers such as vultures and beetles. Their remains fertilise plants, and so the cycle is complete (see right).

The guanaco lives in the Andes mountains of South America.

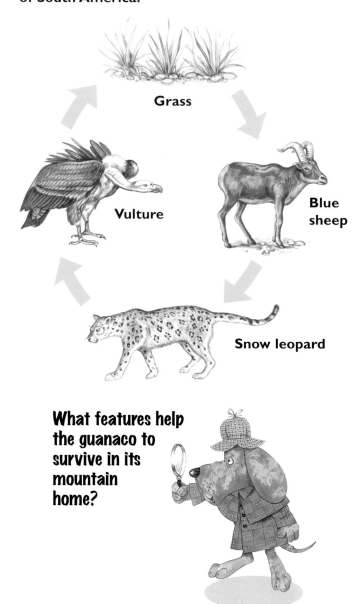

Grass

Vulture

Blue sheep

Snow leopard

DETECTIVE WORK

Use the Internet or your local library to find out about all the animals found in hills or mountains close to where you live. Draw a food chain to show the relationships between the animals. To find out more, go to:

weblinks

www.waylinks.co.uk/series/
GeogDetective/Mountains

What features help the guanaco to survive in its mountain home?

How do we use mountains?

Mountains are useful to humans. Natural resources may include valuable **minerals** such as gold, silver, iron, coal or copper. In North and South America, many mountain towns grew up at sites where gold or silver was found. When the minerals were used up, some of these settlements became abandoned 'ghost' towns.

Building materials such as granite, slate and marble are also **quarried** from mountains. Mining and quarrying often harm the environment. Waste heaps of rock called 'spoil heaps' are left around the mine.

Forests that grow on the slopes of mountains are also valuable resources. They are harvested for timber or to burn wood as fuel. However, the roots of forest trees hold the soil in place on steep slopes. When trees are cut down the soil becomes loose, and can wash away after heavy rain. In some places, such as Nepal in the Himalayas, whole hillsides have collapsed after forests have been chopped down.

Silver has been mined on this mountain in the South American Andes, called Cerro Rico, for hundreds of years. However, nothing will grow on the spoil heaps.

Streams flowing from the mountains provide water for the **lowlands**. Streams are often dammed to create artificial lakes called **reservoirs**. The energy of rushing streams can also be harnessed to generate electricity. This is called **hydroelectric power** (HEP). Streams are often dammed when HEP plants are built. HEP does not pollute the environment, but dams and reservoirs change the natural world, destroying wild habitats. Sometimes villages or even towns are moved to make way for reservoirs.

DETECTIVE WORK

Find out more about the advantages and disadvantages of generating hydroelectric power in mountain areas. For more information, go to:

weblinks

www.waylinks.co.uk/series/
GeogDetective/Mountains

This HEP plant has been built on a river in California, USA. A lake has formed behind the dam.

How do people live in mountain areas?

Mountain areas usually have fewer towns and villages than **lowlands** because of the hostile **climate** and the difficulties of living on slopes. Most settlements grow up in sheltered valleys below the peaks, usually on the side that catches the morning sun. Some villages are located on shelves above the main valley to avoid flooding in spring. People also build away from sites that are at risk of landslides and **avalanches** (see pages 24-25).

DETECTIVE WORK
Find a tourist brochure of a mountain resort with photos and a map of the region. Can you explain why the resort has grown up there?

The Swiss town of Lauterbrunnen lies on the sunny side of a deep valley carved by ice.

Mountain homes are designed to be warm and comfortable in cold weather. They are usually built of local materials such as stone or timber, with roofs of slate or tiles. In the Alps, traditional buildings had several storeys where people lived on the first floor and animals were kept on the ground floor in winter. The body heat of the animals helped keep people warm. Hay stored in the loft provided **insulation**. Many modern buildings are fitted with triple glazing, which keeps the heat in.

Until recently many mountain villages were isolated in winter. They might be cut off by snow for months, so local people had to be self-sufficient. These remote villages were often the last places to get electricity, piped water, schools and doctors' surgeries. Nowadays, many houses have electricity and are linked to the wider world by radio, telephone and the Internet. Places that rely on tourism have efficient transport links with the outside world.

This traditional mountain home in Austria is made of local materials such as wood, stone and slate.

Why are floods common in mountain regions in spring?

What work do people do?

The main work for mountain people has traditionally been farming. However, farming in the highlands can be difficult because of the cold, wet **climate** and poor soil. Steep slopes also make farming difficult. Farmers often cut steps called terraces into hillsides to create flat land. Fields are tilled using ploughs drawn by donkeys or oxen, and animal dung is used to fertilise the soil.

Where the climate is too harsh to grow crops, farmers raise animals such as cattle, sheep, goats or llamas for meat, milk, hides or wool. In spring, the animals are taken up to the high **pastures**. They are brought down again for the winter months.

Farmers plant rice on terraces in Longji, China.

Tourism has now overtaken farming as the main industry in many mountain regions. In summer, tourists arrive to go hiking, biking, fishing or climbing. In winter, they come for skiing and snowboarding.

Tourism has changed the way of life in many mountains for ever. Villages that were once quiet are now bustling resorts. Tourism brings new work for local people, who run shops, hotels and restaurants, work as guides or porters, or make crafts to sell as souvenirs.

Ski resorts bring changes to mountain areas. New roads are built and safe slopes called pistes are prepared.

FOCUS ON

Tourism on Everest

Namche Bazaar is the highest small town in the Everest region. Once busy only on market days, it now welcomes walkers and climbers on their way to Everest. Western-style restaurants, lodges and even Internet cafés have transformed this remote mountain settlement.

In the Himalayas, porters help carry supplies for mountain trekkers.

Why is travel difficult in mountain areas?

The steep terrain and harsh weather in mountain regions make travel difficult. In days gone by, the only way to travel was on foot, using pack animals to carry loads. Narrow, stony trails wound up to high passes that were only open in summer. Remote regions such as the Himalayan kingdoms of Nepal and Bhutan still have very few roads.

Nowadays, efficient roads and railways make travel easier in areas such as the Alps and Rocky Mountains in North America. Mountain roads have many hairpin bends which make the climb more gradual. Bridges span rivers and deep **gorges**, while in some areas, tunnels have been blasted right through the mountain. Heavy snow in winter can still be a problem. Bulldozers work to clear some routes, while others close until spring.

Yaks are still used for transport in the Himalayas.

Tourism has led to improved transport in many mountains. Ski-lifts and cable cars carry skiers and sightseers up to the high slopes. Mountain railways bring tourists to summits such as Snowdon in North Wales and the Jungfrau in Switzerland. New airports built near the mountains allow large numbers of tourists to visit. Helicopters are used to bring supplies to remote villages and to rescue injured people.

DETECTIVE WORK
Study the photograph of Chamonix and go to the library to find out more about the town. Draw a map showing Chamonix's transport network. How has the tunnel helped to overcome the problems of travelling around the mountain?

FOCUS ON

Transport links for Chamonix

Chamonix, in the shadow of Mont Blanc in the French Alps, is a centre for mountain tourism. Cable cars carry tourists to peaks above the town. In the nineteenth and twentieth century, efficient roads and a railway were built to link Chamonix with other parts of France and with Switzerland. In the 1960s, a tunnel was blasted right through Mont Blanc to connect with Italy.

This view of Chamonix shows the layout of the town on the valley floor and a cable car that carries tourists up the mountain.

Are mountains dangerous?

Mountains can be dangerous places. People who are not used to the thin air high on mountains may feel dizzy, sick, or get a headache: all signs of **altitude sickness**. The only cure is to go lower down. Icy weather brings the risk of frostbite, which can damage toes and fingers. Howling winds and heavy snowfall may combine to form blizzards.

Flash floods can be a problem if the snow melts quickly in spring. Mountain streams become raging torrents, which can sweep trees and bridges away! Landslides and **avalanches** are a danger on steep slopes. A landslide is when a huge mass of earth and rock slips away at once. An avalanche is a similar slide of snow. Avalanches are sometimes set off by earthquakes. In 1970, an earthquake on Mount Huascaran in the Andes triggered an avalanche which killed over 20,000 people in the valley below.

Rocks fall down a mountain slope towards a village during an avalanche in Switzerland.

DETECTIVE WORK

Using the library and the Internet make a map of the disaster zone around Mount St Helens. Use a different colour to mark the danger zone in which you think it would be unsafe to build in future. To find out more information, go to:

weblinks

www.waylinks.co.uk/series/
GeogDetective/Mountains

In 1980, Mount St Helens volcano, USA, exploded. 130,000 acres of forest land were destroyed by landslides and 57 people died.

People living on the slopes of volcanoes are in danger if the volcano erupts, sending red-hot **lava**, ash and burning gases spilling down the mountain. In 1985, an Andean volcano called Nevado del Ruiz erupted. Hot ash falling on snowy slopes started a mudflow which raced down the mountain, burying a town called Armero, and 23,000 people died.

How can we take care of mountains?

Mountains may look indestructible, but in fact, they are delicate habitats that are easily damaged by humans. Mining and dam-building can change these environments, while the cutting of forests can cause **erosion**.

A stone path is laid in the Brecon Beacons, Wales, to prevent erosion from hikers' feet.

Tourism can bring pollution and erosion. Visitors may leave litter, such as toilet paper and even oxygen cylinders, on peaks such as Everest. Hikers and skiers trample plants, while too many visitors can frighten animals.

Mountains can be harmed by distant pollution. The world is getting warmer because of pollution that results when we burn coal, oil and gas for energy. This problem, called **global warming**, is causing mountain **glaciers** to melt, which is changing mountain habitats.

Recently people have realised how important it is to look after wild places such as mountains. Work of this kind is called conservation. In many different countries, mountains have been protected by being made part of national parks and reserves, where it is forbidden to harm animals, pick flowers or leave litter. Park wardens work to prevent erosion and protect wildlife.

What clues suggest that the glacier is getting smaller?

This glacier in the Alps is melting as the climate gets warmer.

Your project

If you've done all the detective work and answered Sherlock Bones' questions, you now know a lot about mountains! This information will help you produce your own project about mountains.

First you'll need to choose a topic that interests you. You could take one of the topic questions below as a starting point.

Cycling is a good way to enjoy mountain scenery without damaging the environment.

Topic questions

- Find out all you can about life in the mountain nearest to where you live. Do people there still earn their living by working in traditional jobs such as farming, or do they now do different kinds of work?

- Compare the way of life in two mountain settlements, for example a remote village in the Himalayas and a modern resort in the Alps.

- What forces have formed and shaped your nearest mountain, or another mountain **range** of your choice?

- Find out about the plants and animals that live in the mountain nearest to you. Are human activities changing the mountain habitat, and if so, what conservation work is being done to preserve it?

Your local library and the Internet can provide all sorts of information to help you find out more. You could present the information in an interesting way, perhaps using one of these presentation ideas.

Sherlock Bones has done a project about dogs that work in the mountains. He has discovered that some dogs protect sheep or goats from predators such as wolves and bears, while others help rescue people in difficulties.

In the Scottish highlands, snow hares change colour with the seasons to hide from enemies. In summer, their brown fur merges with the heather. In winter, their white coat blends in with the snow.

Project presentation

- Make a map of your chosen mountains in the middle of a large piece of paper. Show the summits, villages, rivers, roads, and railways of the region. Stick photos or pictures around the map showing local wildlife, or the mountain at different times of year.

- Imagine you are making a TV documentary about life in the mountains. Draw a diagram with headings for the major points you want to make and explain all about life in the mountains to viewers who know nothing about the area.

- Imagine you are a mountain dweller such as a shepherd, ski instructor, park warden, miner, porter or rescue worker. Write about your life and how it changes throughout the year.

Glossary

Altitude sickness A term used to describe the ill-effects of dizzyness, sickness and headaches felt by people who are not used to the lack of oxygen high up on mountains.

Avalanche A falling mass of snow and rock.

Climate The long-term weather conditions in a region.

Condense When water changes from a gas into a liquid.

Corrie A small, round lake that forms where ice wears a bowl-shaped hollow in the mountains.

Crust Earth's outer layer.

Erosion When rock or soil is worn away and carried off by wind, ice or flowing water.

Fault A deep crack in rocks near the Earth's surface. Faults are often found near the borders of tectonic plates.

Fault-block mountain A type of mountain formed when a block of land is forced upward between two faults running side by side.

Fold mountain A type of mountain that forms where land is forced upward between two tectonic plates that are pressing together. The rocks buckle upward into folds.

Frostbite Damage to the body caused by extreme cold.

Glacier A large mass of ice slowly flowing downhill.

Global warming The gradual warming of the Earth's atmosphere as a result of greenhouse gases, such as carbon dioxide, trapping heat.

Gorges Deep narrow valleys worn by a stream or river.

Gullies Channels worn by running water.

Hydroelectric power (HEP) Electricity that is generated using fast-flowing water.

Insulation A material that prevents heat from escaping into the air.

Lava Hot, melted rock which wells up from underground onto the Earth's surface.

Lowlands Low-lying areas that are only a short distance above sea level.

Minerals The non-living substances from which rocks are made.

Molten When something is semi-liquid, such as hot volcanic rock.

Moraine A mass of rocky debris dropped by a glacier.

Pastures Areas where the main form of vegetation is grass.

Quarrying When stone is mined from the surface of the ground. The stone is usually used in construction.

Rain shadow An area that is dry because a mountain shields it from moist winds.

Range The name given to a group of mountains.

Reservoir An artificial lake created by a dam and used to store water.

Sacred When a place is thought to be holy.

Scree Piles of loose rock that build up at the foot of mountain slopes.

Tectonic plate One of the giant rocky slabs that make up the Earth's crust.

Tuber Part of a plant that is used to store nourishment and is found underground.

Answers

Page 5 A height gain of 3,800 m with a fall of 1°C for every 150 m gives a total temperature loss of 25°C. If the temperature in the valleys is 32°C, the summit temperature is around 7°C.

Page 7 Volcanoes that erupt thick, sticky **lava** build up into tall, cone-shaped peaks such as Mount Fuji. Volcanoes that erupt runny lava form lower, more rounded mountains.

Page 9 Red Tarn below Helvellyn is a **corrie** lake, carved by ice.

Page 10 You need to take warm, waterproof clothing such as raingear, a fleece jacket and woolly hat, also light clothing in summer. Don't forget your suncream and sunglasses or a wide-brimmed hat.

Page 15 The guanaco has dense fur to provide insulation against icy mountain winds. It also has large lungs to take in more oxygen.

Page 19 Flooding occurs mainly because of snowmelt.

Page 27 You can see the line of loose rock and soil, called **moraine**, left by the glacier as it flowed downhill. The ice now ends higher up.

Further Information

Books to read

Geography Fact Files: Mountains
by Anna Claybourne
(Wayland, 2004)

Habitats: Mountains
by Robert Snedden
(Franklin Watts, 2004)

The Mountain Book
by Brian Knapp
(Atlantic Europe Publishing, 2000)

The Mountain Environment
by Clare Hibbert
(Evans Brothers, 2005)

Websites:

http://en.wikipedia.org/wiki/Mountains
This gives you lots of facts about the characteristics of mountains.

www.mountainpartnership.org
Looks at the importance of mountains and how global warming will affect them.

www.mountainvoices.org
Contains interviews with mountain-dwellers.

Index

The Geography Detective Investigates

Contents of all books in the series:

WAYLAND